Sound

Contents

Revision

Did you know. . ?

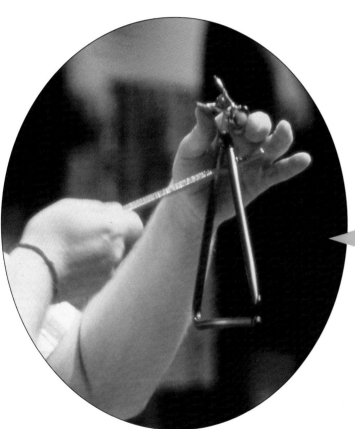

There are lots of different sounds. We hear sounds with our ears.

We can make sounds in different ways. Sound is made when something vibrates.

Sounds can be loud. Sounds can be quiet. Sounds get quieter the further they go.

⭐ **Sounds can be high and sounds can be low.**

⭐ **Sound travels in all directions. Sound can travel through materials.**

Task 1 *Different sounds*

....

✦ Look at the photographs.

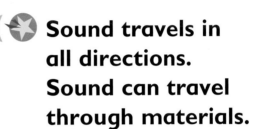

✦ Read these questions.

✦ Write down your ideas.

Which are the loud sounds?
Which are the quiet sounds?
What would you hear if you ran away from the sounds?

Can you think of some musical instruments which make low sounds?
Which musical instruments make high sounds?

Look at the things that make loud sounds. How could you escape from the noise?

⭐ Things which vibrate very quickly are sources of sound.

All these things make sounds.
They make a sound when they **vibrate**
- when they quiver or shake very quickly.

You can feel the vibrations from all these things and from other things as well.

You can feel a piano quiver.

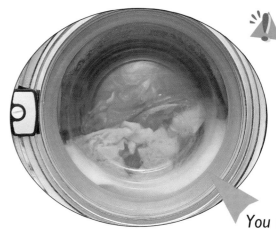

You can feel a machine hum.

You can feel a cat purr.

You can feel your throat vibrate.

 Task 2 *Testing, testing*
....

🔆 Try putting a pencil against things that make a sound.

🔆 Feel the vibrations through the pencil.

Always use the same pencil.
Always hold it in the same way.
Feel the vibrations.

🔆 Draw and write to show the things you try.

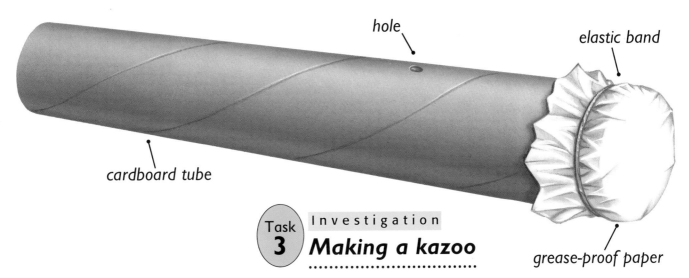

hole

elastic band

cardboard tube

grease-proof paper

Making a kazoo

·····························

A kazoo is a musical instrument.
Make a kazoo like the one shown in the picture.

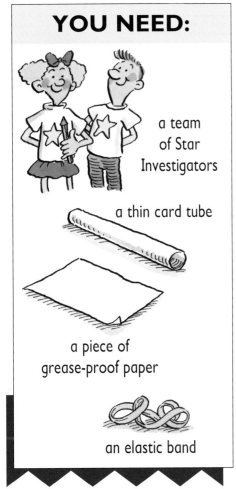

YOU NEED:

a team
of Star
Investigators

a thin card tube

a piece of
grease-proof paper

an elastic band

✦ Hold the paper over the tube end with
the band.
Put the grease-proof paper over one end
of the tube. Hold it in place with the elastic
band. Make a small hole in the tube.

✦ Hum into the open end.
Feel the grease-proof paper.
It vibrates.
It makes your hum into a buzz.

✦ Can you change the buzz?
Try using longer and shorter tubes.

✦ Use a planning board to help you plan
your investigation.

✦ Was this a fair test?
Were the tubes
- the same material? the same width?
Did you keep your hum the same?

✦ Make a table like this to show what
happens.

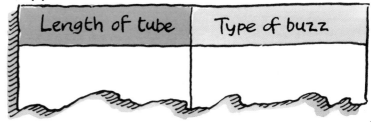

PLANNING BOARD

Our question.
We will change.
We will measure.
We will keep
these things the
same to make
our test fair.
This is the
table we will
use.
(Put in the
headings. Fill
in the left-hand
column)
We will use
these things

Length of tube	Type of buzz

✦ What did you find out?

Seeing vibrations

 Write down some words that would describe the sounds made by these things.

dropping a brick!

a wall falling over

a crashing car

your class jumping off the hall stage together

an elephant sitting on a school chair

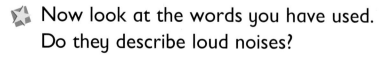 Now look at the words you have used. Do they describe loud noises?

What is vibrating? It's hard to see! Things that vibrate quickly are sources of sound. But you can't always see the vibrations. They are too small!

How to see invisible vibrations

There is a way of seeing vibrations.

✪ Strike a tuning fork on a table top (1).
The tuning fork vibrates and gives
out a note.
But you can't see it vibrating!

✪ Strike the tuning fork on the table again.
Hold the fork up against a bright light (2).
Can you see the vibrations now?

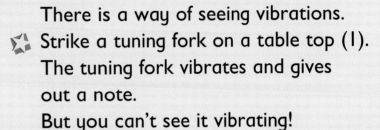

✪ If you press the end of the tuning fork to
the table, the table top **amplifies**
(increases) the sound.
But you still can't see the sound.

✪ Tape a table tennis ball to a thread,
and hang the ball up, or ask someone
to hold it.

✪ Now strike the tuning fork against the
table again.

✪ Bring the vibrating fork up against the
ball (3). Watch what happens.

You aren't hitting the ball. What makes
the ball jump?

✪ Now put the vibrating fork into water (4).
What happens?
Can you explain what is going on?
Draw and write to show your ideas.

Task 6 Beat that drum!

You can't see a drumskin vibrate.
But there is a way of finding out if the drumskin vibrates.

 Scatter some rice on the drumskin.
Beat the drum. Watch what happens.

Now try picking up the drum, with the rice on top.
Beat the other drumskin underneath the drum. What happens?

Task 7 Investigation Puzzle

Put a long plastic ruler over the edge of your desk.
Lean on the end to hold it down.
Push the end down.

Twang the ruler. Can you see the vibrations?

Change one thing to change the speed of the vibrations.

Record your results on the table on Photocopy Master 3.

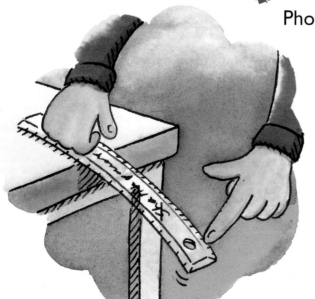

Use numbers in the first column on your table.
Clue: the markings on the ruler might help you.

Seeing sound

You can hear the sounds made by tuning forks, elastic bands and rulers, even if you can't see them. There is a way to see the sounds you make when you speak.

How to make a soundscope:

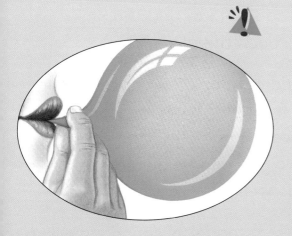

✪ Ask your teacher to blow up a big balloon before you start.

✪ Let the balloon down by untying the end - or you could prick the balloon at the stem end. (What makes the noise?)

✪ Now ask your teacher to take both ends off a small tin.
Watch out for sharp edges.

✪ Cut out a large circle of rubber.

✪ Stretch the rubber circle over the tin. Ask someone to hold it there with an elastic band.

✪ Glue a scrap of cooking foil near the centre of the circle.

✪ Catch the sunlight on the foil. Reflect it on to a shaded wall.

✪ Now speak, sing, or play an instrument near the open end of the soundscope.

✪ How can you make the spot of light move faster?
How can you make the spot of light move further?

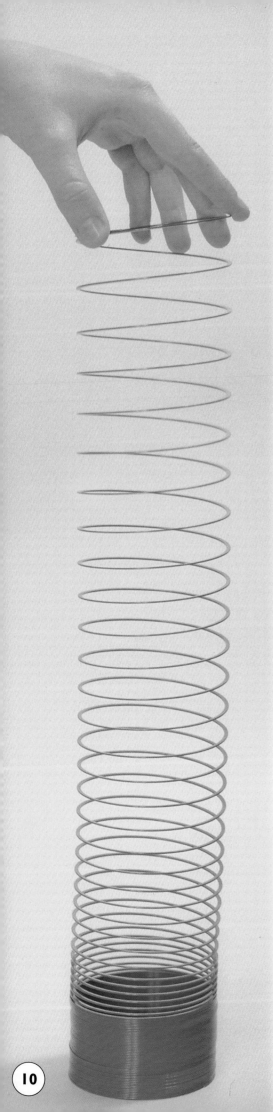

What is sound like?

You can't see sound.
But you can make models of how
it travels.

 Lift the top coils of a Slinky to make it
stretch.

 Let the coils go.
At the same moment, say your name.
The wave that goes down the coil is
rather like the sound of your name,
travelling through the air.

But the sound of your name doesn't come
out of your mouth and fall on the floor!
People all around you can hear it.
People above you and below you can hear
you speak as well!

 You can make a model of sound travelling.

YOU NEED:

an orange

toothpicks

 Push the sticks into the orange
- all over it, so that they face in
every possible direction.

This model shows how sound travels out
from you.

YOU NEED:

a team of Star Investigators

a playground

something that makes one noise:
a bell, a triangle,
a small drum or a cymbal

Task 10 Investigation
Which way did it go? PCM 4.5.6

Ready? Here's the question:

How can you prove that sound travels in all directions?

PCM 4

✦ Discuss this with your team.

✦ Draw some pictures to show how sound travels in all directions.

✦ **Predict** what will happen if you ring a bell in the middle of the playground.

✦ How can your team help you?
What should they **observe**?
What should they **record**?

 PCM 5

✦ When you have planned your investigation, share your plan with your teacher. Is your plan safe and sensible? Use a planning board to help you. (See page 5).
Try it. What happens?

✦ Could you stop sound going in all directions?
How would you do it?
What could you change?
What must you keep the same?

 PCM 6

✦ How could you prove that sound travels up and down as well as around?
Plan a test, and share it with your teacher.

⭐ **Some materials let sound through them. Some materials do not let sound through them. Some materials reflect sound.**

Task 11 **Does sound come through everything?**

PCM 7

Look at the pictures.
What is happening?
Write about your ideas.

I'll stop the sound for you!

Quick, we won't hear it round this corner

Curses! The sound is coming through the keyhole.

It's all right! I sing much more quietly with my hands over my ears!

YOU NEED:

a tuning fork

string

PCM
8

 Strike the prongs of a tuning fork hard on the desk, and then hold the handle against the wall.
You can hear the wall vibrating, even though the fork makes little noise at all.

 Try it again. This time, hold the fork handle against the back of your hand.
Can you feel the fork vibrating?
Can you hear the sound it makes?

 Now tie your fork in the middle of a metre of thin string.
Hold the ends of the string against your ears - not in them.

 Swing the fork against the table edge, and listen. What do you hear through the string?

You know already that sound travels through the air.

You have made vibrations in the wall, the bone in your hand, the fork and string.

What have you found out?

Now try this

Task 13 *What do you hear?*

....

 Cover your ears.
Suppose a friend put a piece of wood against your cheek-bone, and held the vibrating tuning fork to the end.
Do you think you would hear it? How?

 Write about your ideas.

Task 14 *Out and about*

....

 Run a ruler along some railings.
Ask a friend to listen at the other end of the railings.
Ask your friend to listen again with his or her head to the railings.
What does your friend notice?

Fact File

Beethoven

Ludwig van Beethoven was a composer. He died over 150 years ago. People still enjoy his music today. For the last 20 years of his life, he became more and more deaf.

But Beethoven went on writing music. He nailed a piece of wood to his piano, and gripped it in his teeth. Through the wood, he could hear the music he was writing.

Task 15 — *Silencing sound*

- ✦ Find something that makes a sound.

- ✦ Put it in a box.
  See if you can silence the sound.

- ✦ Now try wrapping the object or radio in different materials.
  Try cloth, paper, and bubble-wrap.
  Try other wrapping materials.

- ✦ Which materials do not let sound through?
  Are they soft materials?

YOU NEED:

something that makes a sound - for example, a kitchen timer, or a battery radio

some different materials - for example, cloth, paper, bubble-wrap

Fact File
Thunder *and* lightning

The noise of thunder, and the flash of lightning, are made at the same moment. But the sound is much slower in reaching you than the light. You see the flash before you hear the rumble.

There is a way of finding out how far away the storm is.

Count the seconds between the flash and the bang. Divide the number of seconds by 3. So, 15 seconds between the flash and the crash means the storm is 5 kilometres away.

15

Now try this

Task **16** *Thunderstorm*

 Look at the Fact File on page 15.
How can you tell whether a storm is
getting nearer, or moving away?

PCM 9

 Try the activity on Photocopy Master 9.

Task **17** *Sounds travel through liquids*

This task is to compare sound travelling
through air and through water.

 Ask your teacher to blow up a balloon.
Put it against your ear.
Ask a friend to put a vibrating tuning
fork against the other side
of the balloon.
Listen to the vibrations.

 Now take another balloon.
Fill it with water. Put it
against your ear. Ask
a friend to put a vibrating
tuning fork against the other
side of the balloon.

PCM 10

 Is this a fair test?
Why should you use:
• the same tuning fork?
• the same sort of balloon?
Why should you try to make both balloons
the same size?

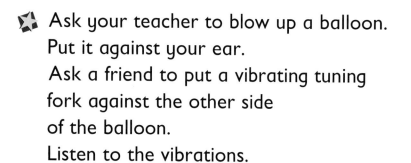

Use Photocopy Master 10 to show your ideas.

Fact File

Dolphins *and* whales

Some of the most amazing sounds in the world are made under water. Sea mammals - like dolphins and whales - call to each other. Their sounds are strong and clear. The sounds can be heard many miles away. This is because sound travels so well through water.

These sounds are called the whale's song.

YOU NEED:

a really quiet place

SHHHH!

A REALLY QUIET ROOM

a ticking clock

a tape measure or a long ruler

You need a really quiet place!

✴ Put a ticking clock on the end of a table.

✴ Measure how close you got before you heard it.

✴ Now put your ear on the far end of the table.
Listen again.

✴ Measure how close you got before you heard the clock.
Surprised? You should hear the clock better through the table than through the air.

▶ **Now try this!**

In outer space, no one can hear you SCREAM

✴ This chilling sentence was used to advertise a science fiction film.
But is it true?
Outer space is very nearly empty.
Without something to travel through, sound can't go anywhere.

✴ Would these astronauts hear each other in space? What might happen if their helmets touched? Draw and write to show your ideas.

YOU NEED:

a ticking watch

a metre ruler

Task 19 How far do sounds travel through solids?

⬖ How could you use a ticking watch and a metre ruler to investigate how far sound travels through solids?

PCM 11

⬖ Draw a plan of what you will do.

⬖ Show your teacher. Carry out your test, and share the results with other people.

Fact File

Feeling the vibrations

Evelyn Glennie is a percussion player. Evelyn can get a rhythm out of anything, for example, coat-hooks, a bed rail, a cheese grater, car exhaust pipes. Evelyn lost her hearing as a child, so she cannot hear the sounds she makes. Instead, she feels the sound with her body and brain. She senses the sound within vibrating objects. In 1984, Evelyn received the highest marks ever at the Royal Academy of Music.

Have you ever made a string
telephone?

These children talked about what they
found out about string telephones.

*Making a string
telephone can be
dangerous. You may need
an adult's help.*

*We tied our string to a
paper-clip. That stopped
it slipping through
the hole.*

*You have to whisper.
Some people shouted.
You could hear them without
the telephone.*

*We found how to send a
message round a corner.
You have to keep the string
away from the wall.*

*We experimented
to find the best
string telephone.*

Read what the children said.
Draw and write to show your own ideas
about making a string telephone.

 Task 21 Investigation
Making the best string telephone

 Make a string telephone.
Look at the pictures to help you.
What could you investigate?
What could you change?

 How can you make a better telephone?
Use a planning board to help you (See page 5).

 PCM 12

 If you change the sort of pot you use,
what happens to the sound?
Compare different pots. Keep the string
the same.

 PCM 13

 How will you judge the best telephone?

YOU NEED:

a team of Star Investigators

materials to make your string telephone

Task 22 — Echoes

✦ Think of some places where you might hear a really good echo.
Some might be inside.
Some might be outside.
Write your ideas in a table like this:

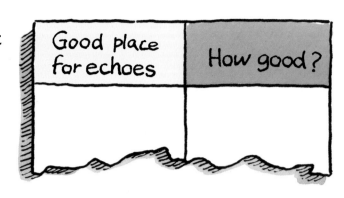

Good place for echoes	How good?

✦ Look at your list.
What is similar about these places?
Have they all got hard surfaces?
List the hard surfaces.

Good place for echoes	This is the hard surface

✦ Is it true to say that hard surfaces make echoes and soft surfaces don't make echoes?

Task 23 — Woks and domes

✦ Have you ever seen a wok?
It's a Chinese frying pan, shaped in a smooth curve.

The wok looks almost like a ball when it's closed.
If you speak into the wok, it echoes your voice back.

✦ Can you guess what happens if you put the two bowls of the wok at each end of a table, facing each other?

✦ Try making different sounds into each bowl. Quiet sounds made in one bowl can be heard near the other.
Don't put your head right in the wok, or it won't work!
Cover the ear that faces away from the wok.

- Ask a friend to snap his or her fingers inside the other bowl.
  Next, try putting your head in the same place, but without the bowl, cover one ear, and try again.

- Science centres use huge bowls like the one in the photograph.
  A person standing in the middle of one bowl can hear a friend in the other.
  One bowl sends the echo to the other.

Fact File

The Whispering Gallery, St Paul's

The huge dome of St Paul's Cathedral works a little like the wok.

If you whisper a message against the wall, a person on the other side of the dome can hear you.

The inside of the dome is called 'The Whispering Gallery'.

These children talked about their library.

Our Headteacher bought a carpet. She put up curtains.

You could hear every chair scrape. Even people whispering sounded loud.

There are no echoes. It's really quiet.

You couldn't work in our library. There was too much noise.

Why do you think the library was quieter?
Why are hard and soft surfaces important?
Draw or write to show your ideas.

Now the library is really quiet. You can think properly.

Before

After

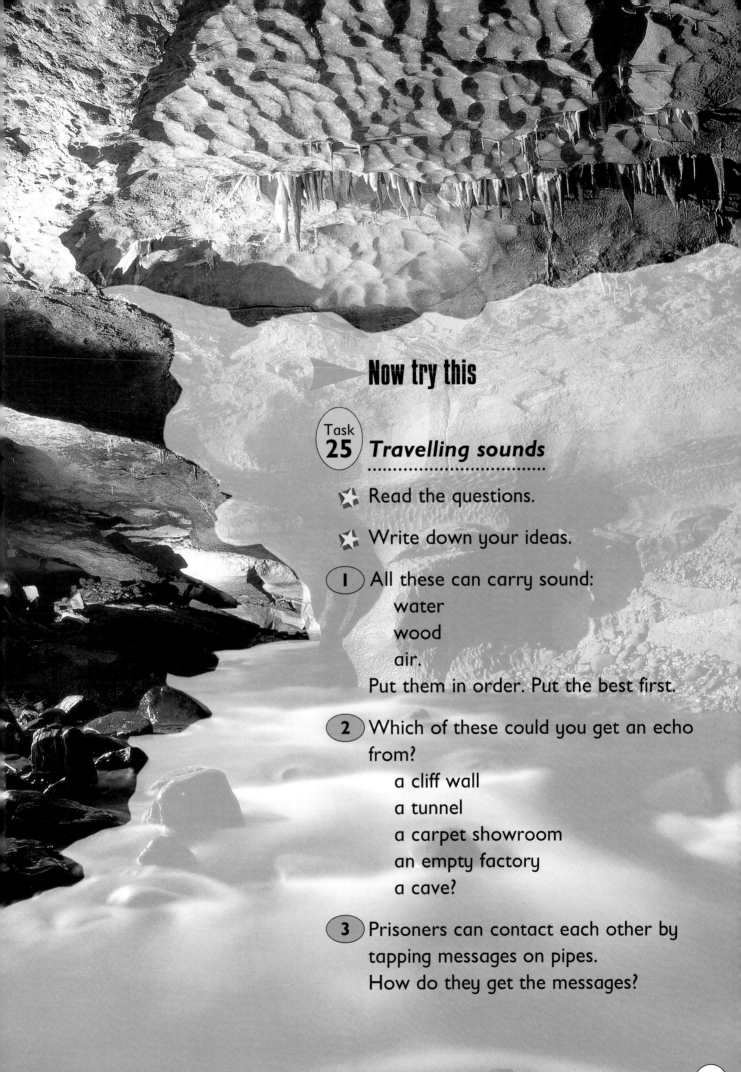

Now try this

Task 25 *Travelling sounds*

⭐ Read the questions.

⭐ Write down your ideas.

1 All these can carry sound:
   water
   wood
   air.
Put them in order. Put the best first.

2 Which of these could you get an echo from?
   a cliff wall
   a tunnel
   a carpet showroom
   an empty factory
   a cave?

3 Prisoners can contact each other by tapping messages on pipes.
How do they get the messages?

We hear things when sound reaches our ears.

These children all have their own ideas about how they hear.

> Well, the sound is whizzing around all over the place, and it reaches my ear.

> When the wind blows, it blows the sound into my ears.

> When I turn my ear towards the sound, my ear sucks all the sound in.

> There's sound everywhere. Some of the sound goes into our ears; that's when we hear it.

Were the children right? What would you tell them about hearing sounds?
Draw and write to show your ideas.

The children were asked the difference between hearing and listening. This is what they said:

You're sort of hearing all the time. But when you really listen, you try to shut out the other sounds.

Sometimes the things on TV are really boring. Sometimes I stop listening to it. But I can still hear it.

I can hear music on my personal stereo. But I really listen to my favourite records.

⭐ How are **listening** and **hearing** different from **seeing** and **watching**?
Can you close your ears? You can stop looking. Can you stop hearing?
Draw and write to show your ideas.

⭐ Now look at Photocopy Master 15.
Which sounds can Big Ears hear?

✦ Look at these animals.

✦ Read the questions.

✦ Draw and write to show your ideas.

You can see the rabbit's ears in the picture. They are like funnels. Why do rabbits keep turning their heads? What do they listen for?

The bat has large ears and tiny eyes. Why do bats need to collect every sound? Why do they listen for the echoes of their squeaks?

The elephant has huge ears. Elephants' ears don't just collect sounds. The elephant uses its ears to lose heat and cool its body. Why is this important?

The song thrush has ears on the side of its head. They are hard to see. How do we know a song thrush can hear? Would birds sing if they couldn't be heard?

The fox's small ears collect sounds from in front. The fox can pick up and follow small sounds. Why does the fox listen like this? What is the fox listening for?

The frog has ears, too. They are on the sides of its head. Why is this? Can frogs hear in the water?

Task
28 *One ear or two?*

Is this true?
**I can tell where sounds
are coming from with one ear, or
with two.**

 Use the blindfold and triangle to try
different ways of testing how you can
tell where sounds are coming from.

 Try the test again or try another test if
you need to.

Finish

THE Sound Game

Play the Snakes and Ladder Sound Game.
Go up the ladders every time a sound travels.
Go down the snakes when a sound is blocked.

Start

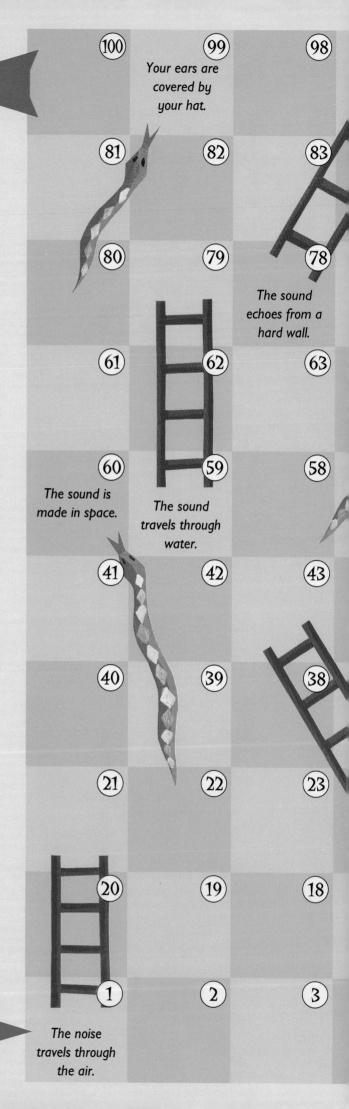

Your ears are covered by your hat.

The sound echoes from a hard wall.

The sound is made in space.

The sound travels through water.

The noise travels through the air.

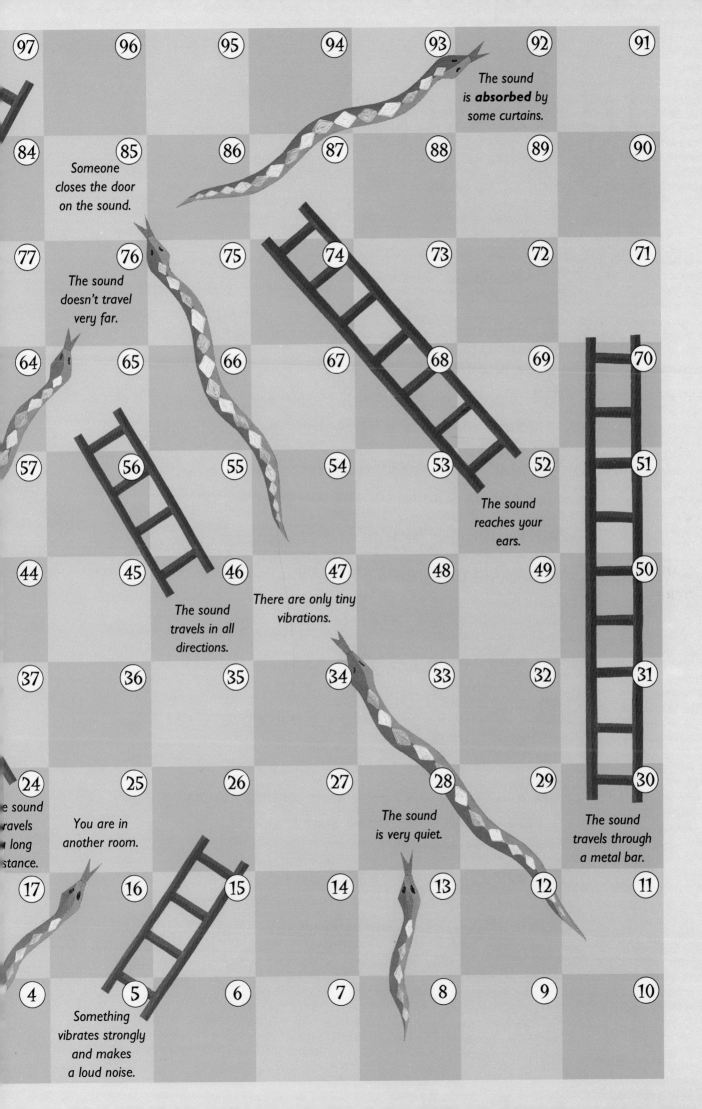

Summary

Revision

★ There are lots of different sounds.
We hear sounds with our ears.

★ We can make sounds in different ways.
Sound is made when something vibrates.

★ Sounds can be loud. Sounds can be quiet.
Sounds get quieter the further they go.

★ Sounds can be high and sounds can be low.

★ Sound travels in all directions.

Key Stage 2 (Lower Junior)

★ Things which vibrate very quickly are
sources of sound.

★ Some materials let sound through them.
Some materials do not let sound
through them.
Some materials **reflect** sound.

★ We hear things when sound reaches
our ears.